Guangdong Paper-cut:
A Wonderland Crafted by Knife & Paper

Elegant Guangdong Series Editorial Board

CONTENTS

Fine Workmanship of Guangdong Paper-cut

Inheritance and Support

Seeking Change through Innovation

Foreword

It would be impossible for anyone visiting Guangzhou Garden Hotel without marveling at the huge golden mural drawn from China's great literary masterpiece *A Dream of Red Mansions* which greets you the moment you step into the lobby. Louis Cha, a martial art novelist, once observed in glowing terms of its stunning artistic effects, "(it feels) as though you are stepping into the Grand View Garden, being transported to the Rong Guo Mansion". Unexpectedly, inspiration for the mural design came from traditional Foshan paper-cut which is of primitive simplicity. It blends perfectly with the hotel design, elucidates with a vengeance the artistic glamour of the outstanding token of Southern China School of paper-cut—the exquisiteness and delicateness of Guangdong paper-cut.

黄飞鸿

Wong Fei-Hong in Lion dance (Foshan paper-cut)

Papermaking is a time-honored business in China. To the Chinese, paper is not only a medium for writing, but also a source of inspiration for artistic creation. Folk art paper-cut is such an art that originates in paper. The history of paper-cut in China goes back to ancient times. It spawned a variety of schools featuring their distinctive styles. Of which, Guangdong paper-cut takes deep root in Lingnan customs and culture, attaining world renown with distinctive characteristics of South China and artistic features.

Foshan School of Paper-cut and Chaoshan School of Paper-cut (referring to areas including Chaozhou or Teochew and Shantou in eastern Guangdong Province) are the best known Guangdong paper-cut schools. The two display distinctly different aspects, as though two flowers engaging in beauty contest. Due to the fact that Foshan paper-cut originated in a town which had a long history of being a trading hub and strong business atmosphere, it had assumed the characteristics of high industrialization, featuring special material and texture, which made it especially known for its magnificence, elegance, splendor and rich local color. Chaoshan Paper-cut originated in the countryside, born out of the variegated folk culture of the area. Clan cultures and folk customs facilitated the birth and development of folk paper-cut as an ornament to folk activities. In the hands of folk craftsmen, it not only instantiates in a variety of styles and forms, but also retains the simple folk customs and the traditional culture of distinctive local color.

Having undergone hundreds of years of ups and downs, Guangdong paper-cut has been on top of the world, and it has also been stuck in slump. In 2006, Guangdong paper-cut became one of the first representative items of national intangible cultural heritage. More than ten years after being selected as an intangible cultural heritage, this ancient art of paper-cut is gradually expanding from the area of being decorative article for folk activities to areas including artwork, urban public space decorative art, which brings forth a fresh look to the inheritance and development of paper-cut in Guangdong. It brings awareness to more people of the exquisite Lingnan culture conveyed by this traditional handicraft, and the timeless charm of Chinese folk arts and crafts.

Lantern parade (Foshan paper-cut)

A Short
Introduction
to Guangdong
Paper-cut

Foshan Paper-cut
Prosperity of Folk Commodities

Chaoshan Paper-cut
Reflection of Folk Customs

Foshan Paper-cut
Prosperity of
Folk Commodities

Origin
A Long History

Foshan has a long history of paper-cut. Foshan paper-cut had already been widely popular in the Song Dynasty (960–1279). It had reached the height of prosperity during the Ming and Qing Dynasties (1368–1911), and it has since developed for over a thousand years. Unrivalled natural endowments, highly developed cutting and carving instruments, time-honored sculpting technological tradition collectively spawned the Foshan paper-cut which stands out distinctively from the multitudes of paper-cut schools across the country.

Chiseled copper foil paper-cut

Foshan paper-cut can be divided into two major categories according to the materials employed: paper and metal foil. The birth of both could be attributed to Foshan's abundant natural resources. Foshan is a land of plenty for mulberry and silk production. As the production center and distribution hub for Guangdong paper industry in the Song Dynasty, paper products of high-quality and competitive price promoted the growth of Foshan's paper-cut business. Foshan is rich in copper foil resources, which provides sufficient raw materials for the production of metal foil paper-cut capable of airing the fullest local characteristics.

9

Foshan paper-cut is famous for its superb use of knife skills, which relies on well-developed cutting tools and a long tradition of carving craftsmanship. According to the currently unearthed cultural relics, the commonly used tools for paper-cut in Foshan, such as scissors, carving knives and chisels, had already been available in the Han Dynasty (206 B.C.–220 A.D.). Foshan paper-cut craftsmen are good at combining the use of cutting, engraving and chiseling together. They use various carving knives for artistic creation. This technique is similar to that of other Foshan carving arts such as wood carving, jade sculpting and ivory carving.

Chiseling is an exclusive skill in Foshan paper-cut

Prosperity
Thriving Due to Business Activity

Foshan paper-cut business reached its peak time during the Ming and Qing Dynasties, which was closely related to the fact that the then Foshan was a prosperous commercial society with well-developed handicraft industry and variegated folk life.

Since the Song Dynasty, a commercial town began to take shape in Foshan, and became one of the "Four Well-known Towns" known for its thriving commerce by the middle of the Qing Dynasty (1636–1911). Therefore, Foshan paper-cut entered the market as a commodity and a tradition of industrialized management came into being at a very early time. Since the Ming Dynasty (1368–1644), paper-cut has developed into an industry that carried weight and enjoyed a considerable market accordingly. More than 300 employees worked in the industry at the peak of its time in the Qing Dynasty, and paper-cut finally developed into a grand booming industry. The metal foil production industry was particularly prosperous from the Ming Dynasty to the middle of the Qing Dynasty. It was an important source of raw materials for Foshan paper-cut. Hence, Foshan was able to develop paper-cut on metal foil materials.

Paper "carving" craft of Foshan paper-cut

Foshan folks are keen on various activities such as participating in idolatrous processions, offering sacrifices to ancestor, throwing Taoist rituals and Buddhist rituals, as well as traditional festivals such as the Spring Festival, the Qingming Festival, the Mid-autumn Festival and the Double Seventh Festival. Paper-cuts are extensively employed for decoration in such activities and festival. Among them, the folk activity of strongest local flavor is no other than the "Chu Qiu Se", which required a tremendous amount of paper-cuts for decoration. The diversification of folk life and the prosperity of the citizen culture provided a broad consumer market for Foshan paper-cut, and ultimately promoted its production and development.

Regulation
Industrial Tradition

The degree of industrialization of paper-cut in Foshan is so high that it is rarely rivaled by other parts of the country. Aspects including the increasing commercialization and socialization, the technicalization of its handicrafts, the specialization of production, the professionalization of practitioners, and the inception of guilds of Foshan paper-cut have all become manifestations of its distinctively high degree of industrialization.

13

Walking across the Tongji Bridge is a traditional folk activity in Foshan

The early industrialization of paper-cut in Foshan prompted paper-cut craftsmen to continuously innovate their tools and improve their skills. In order to meet market needs for mass production, Foshan paper-cut has developed a paper "carving" technique that can process multiple layers of paper-cut patterns at a time. Paper-cut craftsmen also creatively pioneered introducing many techniques belonging to the realm of Chinese paintings to Foshan paper-cut, and developed it into increasingly sophistication and exquisiteness-oriented craftsmanship and style, which adapted itself to the variegated needs of the market. By the Qing Dynasty, all forms of guilds of Foshan paper-cut were established. The establishment of guilds worked out norms for the production and marketing of Foshan paper-cut, and facilitated the growth and development of paper-cut industry in healthy competition, which has increasingly become a thriving and developed industry.

Hundred Birds and Phoenix (Foshan paper-cut)

Chaoshan paper-cut
Reflection of Folk Customs

Origin
Took Root in the Country

The Chaoshan area has long enjoyed the reputation of "Hometown of A Hundred Crafts", and paper-cut is one of the popular folk arts which displays distinctive local characteristics. Chaoshan paper-cut includes Chaoyang paper-cut and Chaozhou paper-cut, both of which are national intangible cultural heritages. They are rich in local cultural characteristics, and are born from and nurtured in the rich and unique Chaoshan folk customs.

The Gate of Asia Art (Foshan paper-cut)

There is no record evidencing the exact time of the origination of the Chaoshan paper-cut. As Chaoshan has long been held as the "living fossil of the ancient culture of central China", legend has it that its origination is also related to the people who migrated from central China to the Chaoshan area. There had already emerged the custom of holding "paper-cut competition" in the Chaoshan area during the Ming Dynasty (1368–1644). *The Bat*, the earliest extant Chaoshan paper-cut sample, was a product of Yongzheng (1723–1735) period in the Qing Dynasty, which was made with exquisite workmanship. It could hence be inferred that Chaoshan paper-cut has attained a high level of workmanship at least by the Qing Dynasty (1636–1911).

Many types of folk paper-cut are dependent on various folk activities, and Chaoshan paper-cut is no exception. The colorful folk festivals in Chaoshan area since ancient times and the fanatical trend in the area to build clan memorial halls and temples collectively created the cultural environment conductive for the survival and popularization of paper-cut. In the period of a year, there are all sorts of activities such as requital of god, offering sacrifice to ancestor and deity, marriage and festivity. All these activities require their own different types of paper-cut patterns including sacrificial flower, gift flower, pie flower, circular flower for ornament and decoration to set off the atmosphere of festival. Monks and nuns from temples and nunneries, in order to participate in the various folk activities, used to acquire superb paper-cut skills. All these facilitated the prosperity and development of Chaoshan paper-cut unobtrusively.

Category
Varying Decorative Paper-cut According to Varying Subjects

Chaoshan paper-cut originates in daily life, which is the mostly used decoration for folk activities such as festivals, games for requital of god, sacrifices and praying for blessings, weddings and funerals. Rich content and plentiful themes have emerged from such activities, and most of them are auspicious themes including auspicious and jubilant activities, parades of dragon and

Chaoshan paper-cut screen

race of phoenix, celebrating lucky events, career promotion in government and longevity, unbroken continuation of the clan, and the abundance of grains. They are mainly classified into categories such as flowers for offerings, decorative flowers for gift and traditional opera characters.

19

Chaoshan paper-cuts, as decoration for offerings in folk activities, are usually called "flowers for offerings". They are often cut like the image of object including animals, flowers and birds, fruits and vegetables as well as other themes and forms, which can be described as a splendor of varieties and colors, while paper-cut of other forms such as the circular flower and the pie flower, the grapefruit flower for decorating seasonal fruits and cakes, chicken pattern and fish pattern for decorating sacrifice for ancestor, the "happiness" (喜 -shaped pattern) or "double happiness" (囍 -shaped pattern) patterns all introduce appeals of different flavor. The specialty of flowers for offering has also contributed to the emergence artistic features of "where there is a pattern, there is an accompanying purpose which bodes well, and flowers are set in flower in the pattern" in Chaoshan paper-cut.

In Chaoshan paper-cut, opera theme is an important form of rich local characteristics, which is deeply involved with the Chaozhou opera. Many older generation of paper-cut craftsmen had taken their subject matters from the Chaozhou opera, such as the figure, plot, setting. They had also created many paper-cut works in the form of comic strip. Paper-cuts based on opera theme created by master craftsman Jiang Genhe are very representative of this category, vivid and true to life, resembling the artistic effect of shadow puppet form strikingly.

Lion Dance (Foshan paper-cut)

A Good Harvest (Foshan paper-cut)

21

Fine Workmanship of Guangdong Paper-cut

Tools
Doing Magic out of Knife and Scissors

Craftsmanship
Fine Carving and Delicate Chiseling

Tools
Doing Magic out of Knife and Scissors

| Foshan paper-cut

Guangdong paper-cuts are known for their extraordinary characteristics of beauty, exquisite carving and fine chiseling, none of which could be effected without tools and materials rich in local color.

Foshan paper-cut can be classified into four main categories: solid color paper-cut, lining material paper-cut, outline drawing paper-cut, and chiseled copper foil paper-cut. In terms of tool and method of creation, Foshan paper-cut can also be defined as "paper carving", that is creating pattern and shape with burin instead of scissors. In the toolbox of a Foshan paper-cut craftsman, burins and chisels are indispensable tools of strong local flavor.

The burin is thin and sharp, convenient for creating delicate paper-cut products. A craftsman usually carries a whetstone with him so that he can sharpen the burin anytime when necessary. Unlike burin, chisel is a unique species of must-have tools for creating chiseled copper Foshan paper-cut, and it is also called "bead knife" for its tapering shape with the tip resembling a ball. Bead knives are used to shape different decorative patterns of paper-cut according to the arrangement and size of the ball.

The main tools of Foshan paper-cut

The Foshan paper-cut is also particular about the paper used. Foshan has well-developed papermaking and paper dyeing industries since ancient times. The paper is of a great variety, high quality and competitive price. The locally produced dyed paper is vigorous and stable in color, bright and eye-catching, of uniform thickness. It provides plentiful and durable raw materials for Foshan solid color paper-cut, which can keep the paper-cut works bright and beautiful for a long time.

Foshan paper-cut craftsmen also creatively introduced four types of foil paper as paper-cut materials, namely, gold, silver, copper and tin. Of which the use of copper foil (commonly known as "gold paper") is especially common, and several other materials such as copper lining material, copper carving material, copper chisel material came into being, which further developed into metal foil paper-cut of distinctive local color. The appearance of these special materials reinforced the local color of the Foshan paper-cut and fully highlighted the splendor and beauty of materials.

Copper foil

| Chaoshan paper-cut

Chaoshan paper-cut can be divided into four types: solid-color paper-cut, multi-color paper-cut, contrast color carving paper-cut, and outline drawing carving paper-cut. The main tools are scissors, some of which are everyday-use scissors, and some are small sharp-nosed scissors. Among Chaoshan paper-cut, the variety unique to the place, "engraving paper", needs to be engraved with a specially made carving knife, which can produce multiple pieces of product at one time, and is fit for large-scale production.

The paper materials used in Chaoshan paper-cut vary in their own characteristics according to subject or occasion of use. In the past, Chaoshan paper-cut mostly used handmade paper made from bamboo fiber produced in southwestern Fujian. After the foundation of the People's Republic of China, most craftsmen switched to use machine-made wax paper. This type of paper has a glossy surface, and is relatively thick, resistance to ruffle and durable, and the finished paper-cut products using such paper are capable of producing more powerful artistic expression.

Craftsmanship
Fine Carving and
Delicate Chiseling

| Foshan paper-cut

Different from other parts of the country where scissors cutting is the main technique employed in paper-cut, Foshan paper-cut has developed many unique techniques such as cutting, carving, chiseling, outline drawing, painting, lining, and dyeing. Among the various crafts, "carving" is the most important method of paper-cut in Foshan. Carving is mainly based on the consistent low pressure applied, which penetrates the paper to the back. It can cut patterns on more than a dozen layers of paper, and multiple paper-cut patterns can be processed at one time, which is appropriate for mass production.

Carving

Chiseling

29

Chiseling is also Foshan's exclusive paper-cut technique, which has especially "come back to life" in the production of chiseled copper paper-cut in recent years. The craftsmanship of chiseled copper paper-cut is extremely complicated and sophisticated. The process involves a piece of copper foil, a chisel knife. First lightly tap with a mallet, and then chisel in place of carving, connect the chiseled dots into lines, and use the lines to form a picture which combine into various patterns of texture or figure contour. Then the finished pattern is complemented with engraved hollow-outs and finally colored. This unique technique produces chiseled copper paper-cut which integrates the artistic conception of calligraphy and painting and the texture of relief, bringing out rich appeal of the traditional art.

It is these delicate, refined and richly layered craftsmanship that work out the exquisite, colorful, and resplendent artistic characteristics of Foshan paper-cut, making it an outstanding representative of Southern China Lingnan School of Paper-cut.

| Chaoshan paper-cut

Chaoshan paper-cut is known for its exquisite, delicate and refined overall style. At the same time, in the hands of folk craftsmen in different regions, they have developed different types of techniques and styles.

Cut

Engraving patterns on copper foil

There are roughly intaglio, relief and combination of intaglio and relief paper-cut methods. Chaoyang paper-cut is based on the relief paper-cut method. The blank part of the main part is cut off. The picture is composed mainly of slender lines, some lines are as thin as hair while each line remains distinct. The composition is symmetrical and full, the pattern fresh and elegant, slim and transparent. This style is related to the fact that the paper-cutting community of Chaoyang folk paper-cut has long been dominated by women. Paper-cut in Chaoshan is also called "flower reaming". Many Chaoshan women are good at needlework, as they have been practicing scissors skills since childhood.

Opposite to the relief paper-cut method, Chaozhou paper-cut is mainly based on the intaglio method, which cuts small pieces of surface and thin lines from a large area of solid color, and pursues regular symmetry in shape, rounded lines, charm of knife work and high decorativeness.

Among the many types of Chaoshan paper-cut, Raoping's "Big Money" paper-cut stands out distinctively. It is a kind of engraved paper-cut of contrast color, which is mainly used for worshiping deities and ancestors, etc. The outline of the finished work is engraved on gold foil which is modeled after a certain object. It then takes the engraved lines as demarcation lines and applies contrast color blocks according to the varying theme or composition requirements. Highlighted by the gold and silver colors, these bright red and green color blocks complement each other and shine in refulgence, manifesting the features of stately magnificence, bold antiquity of the craft.

Garden Party (Foshan paper-cut)

Dragon-boat Race (Foshan paper-cut)

Inheritance
and Support

Seeking Change
through Innovation

Inheritance
Intangible Heritage Conservation

Innovation
Integration with Architecture

Breakthrough
Flourishing on the Silk Road

Inheritance
Intangible Heritage Conservation

In 2006, Guangdong paper-cut became one of the first representative projects of national intangible cultural heritage. Three years later, Chinese paper-cuts represented by Guangdong paper-cuts and Shanxi paper-cuts were included in the representative list of human intangible cultural heritage by the United Nations.

Chiseled copper foil paper-cut

Chiseled copper foil paper-cut

Since the beginning of the new century, Guangdong paper-cut has embarked on a distinctive development path of "productive protection", among which the "resurrection" of Foshan's chiseled copper paper-cut technique could be justifiably exemplary. Chiseled copper paper-cut is a distinctive variety in Foshan paper-cut, but the technique has been lost for more than 30 years. In 2009, Foshan paper-cut master craftsman Chen Yongcai became the representative inheritor of the representative project of national intangible cultural heritage. It was also in the same year that he and Rao Baolian, his disciple, the provincial representative inheritor of Foshan paper-cut, looked for alternative raw materials and innovated techniques; after repeated exploration and research, they restored the long-lost chiseled copper paper-cut technique. The chiseled copper paper-cut *Foshan's New Eight Views* they completed together vividly reproduced "Foshan's New Eight Views" such as The Ancestral Temple, Xiqiao Mountain, and Qinghui Garden, which is considered as the "resurrection of a lost craft".

Exquisite paper cutting craft

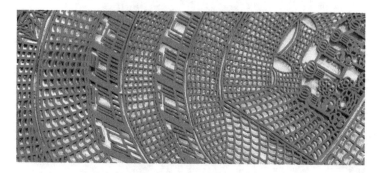

Chaoshan paper-cut was listed as a national intangible cultural heritage at the same time as Foshan paper-cut. The government started a variety of conservation and inheritance work as early as the 1980s, including researching, sorting, and conservation. In 1989, 181 masterpieces (sets) of folk paper-cuts were sorted out, and nearly 500 patterns were included in the book *Folk Paper-cuts of Chaoyang*. In recent years, Chaoshan paper-cuts have been introduced into campuses as textbooks. In 2002, Wei Huijun, the representative inheritor of paper-cut project of the first batch of Guangdong intangible cultural heritage, opened a paper-cut training class in Chaoyang Cultural Center. After that, she served as a paper-cut instructor in a number of primary and secondary schools, and held paper-cut lectures in an effort to widely disseminate paper-cut techniques.

Chaoyang District has been named "Hometown of Chinese Folk Culture and Art" and "Hometown of Folk Culture and Art in Guangdong Province in 2018–2020". Having entered the new century, Chaoshan paper-cut frequently appeared on a variety of art exhibitions. The works of many famous Chaoshan paper-cut craftsmen including Wei Huijun and Chen Yanshu have appeared on major art exhibitions at home and abroad and have won many an important awards, which introduced the unique local art of Chaoshan area to the world.

Innovation
Integration with Architecture

While keeping and transmitting the heritage, Guangdong paper-cut has always been actively looking for a point of integration with contemporary life, and the innovative integration with modern architecture is one of the new attempts.

In 1984, a 22-meter-long and 6-meter-high paper-cut mural *A Dream of Red Mansions—Twelve Beauties in Jinling* was completed and mounted in the lobby of Guangzhou Garden Hotel, which set an exemplary precedent for the combination of paper-cut art and modern architecture in Foshan. In 2003, Chen Yongcai created a large-scale paper-cut mural *Foshan Autumn Splendor Festival* for Foshan Hotel, which once again demonstrated the unique appeal of Foshan paper-cut as a decorative art for modern architectural space.

In recent years, Foshan paper-cut elements have been adopted in the beautification projects of Foshan Metro Station, Xincheng Cultural Center, and Danzao Fairy Lake Park. The new landmark "SWA" erected in Jieyang Chaoshan International Airport is also a public artwork structure with paper-cut elements. These innovative explorations have enabled Guangdong paper-cut to break through the limitations of traditional folk art and made it an large-scale space decoration art of more artistic appeal and more modern sense, which also widens its boundaries and living space.

Paper-cut design at Foshan Tongji Metro Station

The paper-cut mural *A Dream of Red Mansions—Twelve Beauties of Jinling* in the lobby of Guangzhou Garden Hotel

43

Breakthrough
Flourishing on the Silk Road

Thanks to Guangdong's ideal location on the southern coast, well-developed economy and prosperity of commerce, Guangdong paper-cut, especially Foshan paper-cut, has had a long tradition of industrialization and commerce with overseas market. Historically, Foshan paper-cut has been able to travel far to Asian and African countries, as well as Australia, North and South Americas.

Since the 1950s, Foshan paper-cuts have been well sold both at home and abroad. In the early 1960s, paper-cut products designed and created by Foshan Folk Art Research Society were all the rage among the people. In the 1970s and 1980s, Foshan paper-cuts were well received at the "Canton Fair", and it became an "exemplary contributor" to export and making foreign exchange in that era.

Craft master demonstrates the art of paper-cutting

In recent years, Foshan paper-cut and Chaoshan paper-cut have taken on a new look in the process of inheritance. Many inheritors have established paper-cut studios, integrating contemporary arts and crafts design into traditional paper-cut art, and a large number of paper-cut art derivative products have been developed into creative articles in tune with the trend of the time and sold well at home and abroad.

Since the turn of the 21st century, Guangdong paper-cut has not only maintained a prosperous industry momentum all year round, but has also moved from the realm of ancestral halls and temples in the countryside to the refined palace of art. In 2005, Foshan paper-cut became the designated souvenir of the Asian Art Festival. As a characteristic handicraft of Lingnan culture, Guangdong paper-cut has also been frequently admitted to the exhibition halls of professional art galleries and museums, conquering modern audience with its unique artistic charm.

This book is the result of a co-publication agreement between Nanfang Daily Press (CHINA) and Paths International Ltd. (UK)

Title: Guangdong Paper-cut: A Wonderland Crafted by Knife & Paper
Author: Elegant Guangdong Series Editorial Board
Hardback ISBN: 978-1-84464-718-7
Paperback ISBN: 978-1-84464-719-4
Ebook ISBN: 978-1-84464-720-0
Copyright © 2022 by Paths International Ltd., UK and by Nanfang Daily Press, China

Paths International Ltd
www.pathsinternational.com

Published in United Kingdom

CPSIA information can be obtained
at www.ICGtesting.com
Printed in the USA
LVHW020727011222
733371LV00001B/2